QUIZ MAGIC

WRECK-IT RALPH QUIZZES

WHEN THE GAME IS OVER, ... THE FUN BEGINS ...

HEATHER E. SCHWARTZ

LERNER PUBLICATIONS ◆ MINNEAPOLIS

Mark your quiz answers on a separate sheet of paper.
Then check your answers when you're finished with the quiz!

Lerner Publications Company
A division of Lerner Publishing Group, Inc.
241 First Avenue North
Minneapolis, MN 55401 USA

For reading levels and more information, look up this title at www.lernerbooks.com.

Main body text set in Avenir LT Pro 13/16 and ITC Lubalin Graph Std 12/15.
Typefaces provided by Linotype AG and International Typeface Corp.

Library of Congress Cataloging-in-Publication Data

Names: Schwartz, Heather E., author.
Title: Wreck-it Ralph quizzes : when the game is over, the fun begins / Heather E. Schwartz.
Description: Minneapolis : Lerner Publications, [2020] | Series: Disney quiz magic | Audience: Ages 6–10. | Includes bibliographical references.
Identifiers: LCCN 2018045020 (print) | LCCN 2018059919 (ebook) | ISBN 9781541561533 (eb pdf) | ISBN 9781541554740 (lb : alk. paper)
Subjects: LCSH: Wreck-It Ralph (Motion picture)—Miscellanea—Juvenile literature. | Animated films—United States—Miscellanea—Juvenile literature.
Classification: LCC PN1997.2.W74 (ebook) | LCC PN1997.2.W74 S39 2020 (print) | DDC 791.43/75—dc23

LC record available at https://lccn.loc.gov/2018045020
1-45792-42674-1/9/2019

TABLE OF CONTENTS

WRECK-IT RALPH SUPERFAN

HAVE YOU WATCHED THE WRECK-IT RALPH MOVIES OVER AND OVER? Can you quote Vanellope's sassiest lines? Or tell your friends the rules of *Sugar Rush*? You just might be a Wreck-It Ralph superfan!

You've seen Ralph's adventures with Vanellope, Felix, Shank, and all the rest. It's time to gather your friends for some fun of your own. Test your Wreck-It Ralph knowledge with the quizzes in this book.

••ARE YOU MORE LIKE VANELLOPE OR RALPH?

1. Which would you rather do as an afternoon activity?
   A. experiment with new dessert recipes
   B. play with friends

2. In your opinion, potty humor is . . .
   A. super silly
   B. beneath you

3. **Time for a treat! Which would you rather have?**

   A. a chocolate bar
   B. a slice of pie

4. **When a friend tosses you a ball and shouts, "Incoming!" you . . .**

   A. leap to catch it
   B. duck and scream

5. **Oops, you forgot to return a library book. What does that mean?**

   A. The book is late.
   B. You are now a criminal.

6. **Which would you rather ride at an amusement park?**

   A. the roller coaster
   B. the merry-go-round

7. **You have a little money to spend. Which do you buy?**

   A. the newest kind of toy that just came out
   B. another toy like one that is already your favorite

TURN THE PAGE FOR ANSWERS!

COMPARE/CONTRAST

Vanellope and Ralph are great friends, but they are very different. What are some of their biggest differences?

7

YOU ARE MORE LIKE . . .

IF YOU ANSWERED MOSTLY As, you're like Vanellope! You're adventurous and fun-loving. While you don't take life too seriously, you're not afraid of a challenge either.

IF YOU ANSWERED MOSTLY Bs, you're like Ralph! You're super loyal, and friends know they can count on you. You won't let them—or yourself—down.

••VEXING VIDEO GAMES: TRUE OR FALSE?

1. GLITCHES CAN'T LEAVE THEIR GAMES.

2. IF YOU DIE OUTSIDE YOUR GAME, YOU WILL REGENERATE.

3. SECURITY IN GAME CENTRAL STATION ASKS TRAVELERS IF THEY'RE CARRYING VEGETABLES.

4. GOING TURBO MEANS "GOING VERY FAST."

STORYTELLING SPOTLIGHT

A key moment in the plot of *Wreck-It Ralph* is when Vanellope is trapped in the game as *Sugar Rush* is swarmed by Cy-bugs. How would the story be different if she had been able to leave with the others?

1. True. 2. False. If you die outside your game, you will not regenerate. 3. False. Security asks if travelers are carrying fruit. 4. False. Going Turbo means "game-jumping."

RALPH BRAINBUSTER

1. How tall is Ralph?
   A. 7 feet (2.1 m)
   B. 9 feet (2.7 m)
   C. as tall as a skyscraper
   D. as tall as a candy cane tree

2. How much does Ralph weigh?
   A. 150 pounds (68 kg)
   B. about as much as an adult elephant
   C. 643 pounds (292 kg)
   D. the same as Felix

3. Where does Ralph live when his story begins?
   A. with Q*bert
   B. in a garbage dump
   C. under a bridge
   D. in the penthouse

4. Where does Ralph want to live?
   A. in the penthouse
   B. in a garbage dump
   C. in *Hero's Duty*
   D. in a chocolate swamp

5. How does Ralph get his gold coin medal?
   A. by taking it from *Hero's Duty*
   B. by convincing Felix he deserves one
   C. by winning a race in *Sugar Rush*
   D. by helping Vanellope make a race car

STORYTELLING SPOTLIGHT

In early versions of *Wreck-It Ralph*, Felix was the main character. How would the story be different if told from Felix's point of view?

◆WHICH VIDEO GAME WERE YOU BORN TO WIN?

1. Uh-oh! The school bus is driving away without you. What do you do?

A. bike to school with your friend who is also late

B. ask your parents for a ride

C. call out to the driver to turn back

D. catch up with the bus on your roller skates

2. Which animal are you most like?

A. a dog
B. a raccoon
C. a lion
D. a cat

3. Your art teacher passes out directions for a project. You . . .

A. ask permission to work with a friend
B. follow the steps by yourself
C. help classmates do it right
D. make it as creative as possible while still following the rules

4. Pick a sport you'd most like to try.

A. rowing
B. golf
C. soccer
D. snowboarding

5. What would you do if you accidentally broke your little sister's favorite toy?

A. borrow money from friends to buy a new one
B. get out the glue and get to work
C. find a friend to play with your sister as a distraction and another one to help you repair the toy
D. invent a game using the broken pieces

TURN THE PAGE FOR ANSWERS!

STORYTELLING SPOTLIGHT

Each video game is set in a different world. How do the different games reflect their settings? How does the story change based on these different settings?

YOU WOULD BE A MASTER AT . . .

IF YOU ANSWERED MOSTLY As, you'd win *Slaughter Race*! You're a team player who knows winning is important, but friendship ranks even higher.

IF YOU ANSWERED MOSTLY Bs, you'd win *Fix-It Felix Jr.*! Fixing is right up your alley, whether you're cleaning your room or patching a friendship after an argument.

IF YOU ANSWERED MOSTLY Cs, you'd win *Hero's Duty*! You're a strong leader who knows the importance of teamwork. You have the ability to help others succeed.

IF YOU ANSWERED MOSTLY Ds, you'd win *Sugar Rush*! You think—and act—outside the box. You've got your own ideas, and you're not afraid to use them.

VANELLOPE OR SHANK?

1. WHICH CHARACTER TALKS COOL, DRIVES COOL, AND WEARS A COOL LEATHER JACKET: VANELLOPE OR SHANK?

2. WHO STEALS RALPH'S MEDAL TO RACE IN *SUGAR RUSH*: VANELLOPE OR SHANK?

3. WHO SINGS A SONG ABOUT WANTING TO STAY IN *SLAUGHTER RACE*: VANELLOPE OR SHANK?

4. WHICH CHARACTER GLITCHES WHEN SHE'S NERVOUS: VANELLOPE OR SHANK?

5. WHICH CHARACTER ACTS LIKE A BIG SISTER: VANELLOPE OR SHANK?

CHARACTER CONNECTION

Part of being a good friend is being a good listener. Shank is a good listener when Vanellope talks about her problems. How can you be a good listener too?

SUGAR RUSH SUPERFAN SPOTTER

1. Which candy cane branches break?

  A. branches with no stripes

  B. branches with one stripe

  C. double-striped branches

  D. triple-striped branches

2. When are glitches allowed to race?

  A. during practice races

  B. anytime

  C. only when another racer is hurt

  D. never

3. Which racers become the next day's avatars?

A. the first nine racers across the finish line

B. the first five racers across the finish line

C. the racers with the most gold coins

D. the racers with the coolest cars

4. What is the official fee to compete?

A. one stolen gold medal

B. one gold coin from previous winnings

C. two gold coins from previous winnings

D. three gold coins from previous winnings

5. Where do qualified racers get their karts?

A. from King Candy

B. they make them at the Kart Bakery

C. from *Slaughter Race*

D. the karts just appear

CHARACTER CONNECTION

Vanellope knew the rule that kept her from racing was unfair. Being fair is very important in games and in life. When have you seen someone challenge a rule that is unfair?

• HOW LONG WOULD YOU MAKE IT GOING TURBO?

1. What's your favorite place in school?

A. the library
B. the gym
C. the math classroom

2. What would you most like to dress up as for Halloween?

A. a ghost
B. a clown
C. a cat

3. **Would you be willing to shave your head as a disguise?**

  A. Absolutely!

  B. No way.

  C. No, but I'd get a super-short haircut.

4. **Your class is planning a surprise party for your teacher. Would you tell anyone?**

  A. Nope! I'd tell no one.

  B. I'd be so excited I'd have to tell a few friends.

  C. I'd tell only my parents.

TURN THE PAGE FOR ANSWERS!

COMPARE/CONTRAST

What are the similarities between how Turbo acts when he is himself and when he's being King Candy? What are the differences?

YOU WOULD MAKE IT . . .

IF YOU ANSWERED MOSTLY As, congratulations! Looks like you'd do a better job than Turbo himself.

IF YOU ANSWERED MOSTLY Bs, they saw through your disguise right away. But that's OK—there's no reason to hide your true identity!

IF YOU ANSWERED MOSTLY Cs, you almost made it to the finish line. But you weren't quite sneaky enough.

•SLAUGHTER RACE: TRUE OR FALSE?

1. STAYING ON TRACK IS THE ONLY WAY TO WIN.

2. PLAYERS CAN'T USE SHANK'S CAR.

3. A GOLD COIN IS REQUIRED TO COMPETE IN *SLAUGHTER RACE*.

4. SHANK, BUTCHER BOY, AND PYRO ARE ALL RACERS IN *SLAUGHTER RACE*.

COMPARE/CONTRAST

Vanellope likes *Slaughter Race* better than *Sugar Rush*. How are these racing games the same? How are they different?

1. False. Racers can drive anywhere. 2. True. 3. False. There is no entry fee for *Slaughter Race*. 4. True.

21

◆ WHO SAID IT?

1. "All right, ladies! The kitten whispers and tickle fights stop now!"
   A. Calhoun
   B. Felix
   C. Mr. Litwak

2. "Built it myself. Fastest pedal power west of the Whac-a-Mole."
   A. Taffyta Muttonfudge
   B. Vanellope von Schweetz
   C. King Candy

3. "And may you always be just as happy as we wish you to be."

   A. Calhoun
   B. Moana
   C. Merida

4. "I'm bad and that's good! I will never be good, and that's not bad!"

   A. Ralph
   B. Pyro
   C. Shank

5. "I ran higgledy-piggledy all over creation looking for you."

   A. Ralph
   B. Felix
   C. Vanellope

STORYTELLING SPOTLIGHT

Dialogue is one way of learning what's happening in a story. Why is it important to listen to what characters are saying?

GOT WHAT IT TAKES TO SURVIVE HERO'S DUTY?

1. **Which creepy-crawly are you most like?**

   A. a scorpion
   B. a ladybug
   C. a fire ant

2. **Your first rule of *Hero's Duty* is . . .**

   A. "Never interfere with the first-person shooter."
   B. "Save yourself!"
   C. "No cuts, no buts, no coconuts."

3. You toss a dirty shirt into your laundry hamper. It's most likely to land . . .

   A. inside the hamper
   B. next to the hamper
   C. half in and half out of the hamper

4. How would you most like to travel?

   A. by high-speed train
   B. by hot-air balloon
   C. by bike

5. Your brother turns on music while you're reading. What do you do?

   A. keep reading and ignore the music
   B. close your book and start listening
   C. shut the door to muffle the sound

TURN THE PAGE FOR ANSWERS!

CHARACTER CONNECTION

Hero's Duty is all about teamwork. Think about a time when you worked in a team to get something done.

LET'S SEE . . .

IF YOU CHOSE MOSTLY As, you're itching to earn a medal! Follow Sergeant Calhoun into battle, and together you'll come out on top.

IF YOU CHOSE MOSTLY Bs, steer clear of *Hero's Duty*! Try another game where your talents will shine.

IF YOU CHOSE MOSTLY Cs, it's not a sure thing, but you're willing to try. Put in the effort, and you just might make it!

••BREAKING THE INTERNET: TRUE OR FALSE?

1. MR. LITWAK'S WIRELESS INTERNET PASSWORD IS HIGHSC0RE.

2. YESSS IS IN CHARGE OF THE SEARCH BAR.

3. BUZZZTUBE HEARTS ARE WORTHLESS.

4. YOU NEED A PERMIT FOR POP-UPS.

COMPARE/CONTRAST

How is the internet similar to Game Central Station? How are the two different?

1. True. 2. False. KnowsMore is in charge of the Search Bar.
3. False. BuzzzTube hearts can be converted into dollars.
4. True.

MAKE YOUR OWN QUIZ!

READY TO GET CREATIVE? Make your own Wreck-It Ralph quiz! Copy the blank quiz on the next page, and pick a topic. Maybe you want to challenge your friends on how much they know about a particular video game or character. Or you could ask about the different characters in *Sugar Rush*, like the donut cops, cookie guards, and Devil Dogs. It's up to you to play the game the way you want to!

MY

WRECK-IT RALPH QUIZ:

_____

1. _____

   A. _____

   B. _____

   C. _____

   D. _____

2. _____

   A. _____

   B. _____

   C. _____

   D. _____

3. _____

   A. _____

   B. _____

   C. _____

   D. _____

COPY THIS PAGE!

FUN FACTS

Game Central Station was made to look like the railroad and subway station Grand Central Station in New York City.

The high score on *Fix-It-Felix Jr.* is 120,501. It stands for Walt Disney's birthday, December 5, 1901.

Ralph could have been a bulldozer. The crew at Disney had a lot of ideas about how Ralph could look before they decided on his human version.

TO LEARN MORE

BOOKS

DK. *Ralph Breaks the Internet: Wreck-It Ralph 2 Official Guide.* New York: DK, 2018.
This guide is packed with facts and fun info all about the second film in the Wreck-It Ralph franchise.

Loya, Allyssa. *Bugs and Errors with Wreck-It Ralph.* Minneapolis: Lerner Publications, 2019.
Want to know more about coding? Join Ralph and his friends as you explore bugs and errors.

WEBSITES

Ralph Breaks the Internet
https://movies.disney.com/ralph-breaks-the-internet-wreck-it-ralph-2
Explore more about Ralph and Vanellope's latest adventures breaking the internet.

Wreck-It Ralph
https://movies.disney.com/wreck-it-ralph
Play games, watch videos, create crafts, and learn more about *Wreck-It Ralph* characters!